Piano · VOCAL · GUITAR

THE BEST SOUL SONGS EVER

ISBN-13: 978-1-4234-3044-5
ISBN-10: 1-4234-3044-1

HAL•LEONARD® CORPORATION
7777 W. BLUEMOUND RD. P.O. BOX 13819 MILWAUKEE, WI 53213

Visit Hal Leonard Online at
www.halleonard.com

CONTENTS
THE BEST SOUL SONGS EVER

B-A-B-Y

Words and Music by DAVID PORTER
and ISAAC HAYES

Moderate Rock

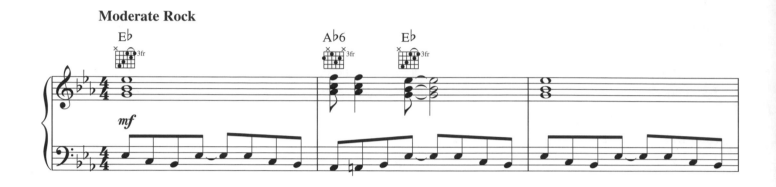

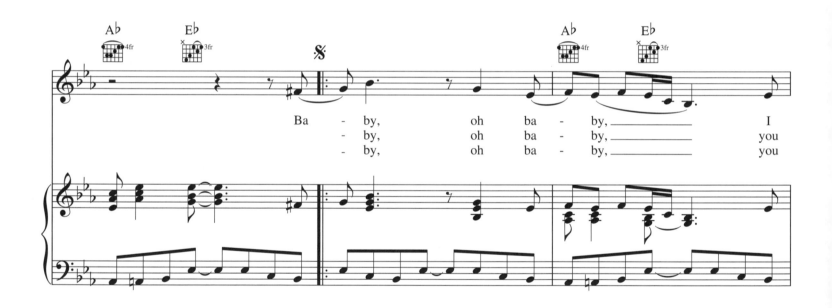

Ba - by, oh ba - by, _____ I
- by, oh ba - by, _____ you
- by, oh ba - by, _____ you

love to call ___ you ba - by. ___ Ba - by, oh ___ ba -
look so good to me, ba - by. ___ Ba - by, oh ___ ba -
look so good to me, ba - by. ___ Ba - by, oh ___ ba -

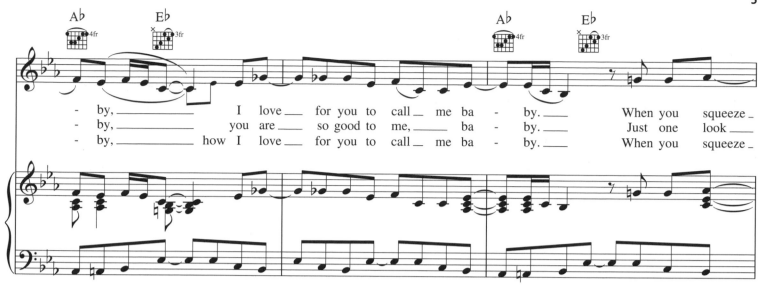

-by, _____ I love ___ for you to call ___ me ba - by. ___ When you squeeze ___
-by, _____ you are ___ so good to me, _____ ba - by. ___ Just one look ___
-by, _____ how I love ___ for you to call ___ me ba - by. ___ When you squeeze ___

___ me real ___ tight, _____ you make _____ the wrong things _
___ in your ___ eyes _____ and my tem - per - a - ture goes sky ___
___ me real ___ tight, _____ you know you make _____ the wrong things _

right. _____
high. _____ And I can't stop lov - ing ___ you, _____
right. _____ I weep for you ___ and can't help ___ it.
And I can't stop lov - ing ___ you, _____

To Coda

BABY I'M FOR REAL

Words and Music by ANNA GORDY GAYE
and MARVIN GAYE

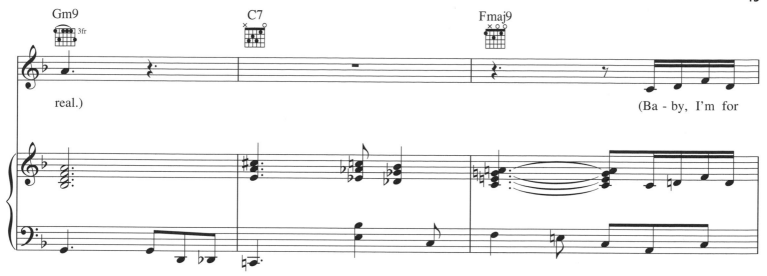

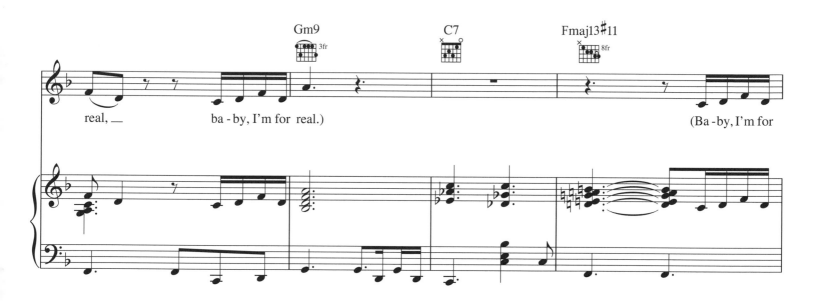

Additional Lyrics

Oh darlin', no, no.
Never, never, never gonna leave you now, baby.
Oh, this is how I feel.
No, baby, oh baby, I'm for real.

BLUES STAY AWAY FROM ME

By ALTON DELMORE, RABON DELMORE,
WAYNE RANEY and HENRY GLOVER

why you keep on haunt - ing me. _____

Blues, _____ stay a - way from
Love _____ was nev - er meant for

me.
me.

Blues, _____ why don't you set me
True love _____ was just a mem - o -

CANDY

Words and Music by ISAAC HAYES
and STEVE CROPPER

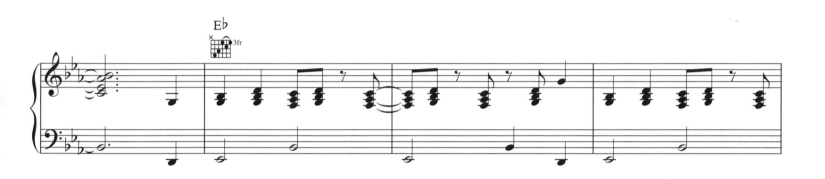

Gee whiz, ah, have you seen my girl?____
wee, she's got a hug so warm.____
whiz, she's got___ ev - 'ry - thing.____

CALL ME
(Come Back Home)

Words and Music by WILLIE MITCHELL,
AL GREEN and AL JACKSON, JR.

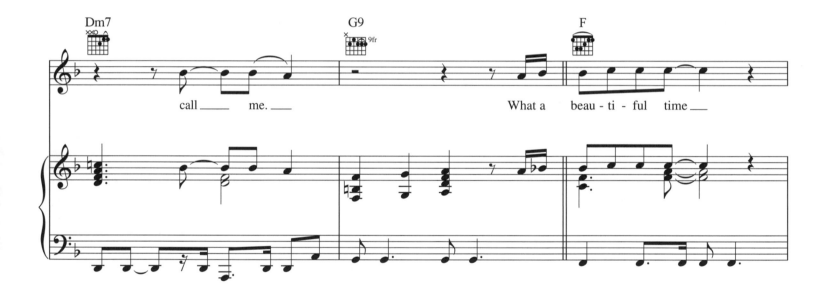

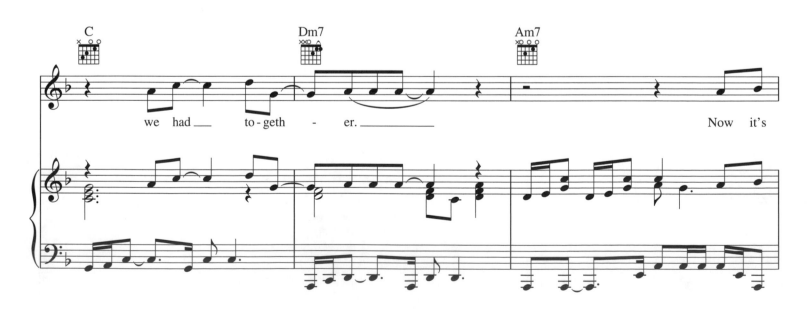

28

CHEAPER TO KEEP HER

Words and Music by
MACK RICE

COME TO MAMA

Words and Music by EARL RANDLE
and WILLIE MITCHELL

If the sun _____ goes _ be-hind the clouds, _ and you fear _____ it's gon-na rain, _____ and if the

THE CHOKIN' KIND

Words and Music by
HARLAN HOWARD

no.   Don't break   your   heart, ba - by,   oh

no.   I   know   you   love   me,   real - ly   I   do,

hon - ey.   I   tell   you your __ love _____ scares me   to death, __

__ girl.   It's   the   chok - in'   kind. _____

CRY BABY

Words and Music by NORMAN MEADE
and BERT RUSSELL

I know she told _____ you, _____
Don't you know, _____

hon-ey, I know she told you that she loved you _____ much more _____ than
hon-ey, ain't no-bod-y ev-er gon-na love you _____ the way _____ I

I, _____ yeah; all I know is that she left you _____ and you
try to do; who'll take all your pain _____ and the

oh, dad - dy, like you al - ways say'n' to do. _____

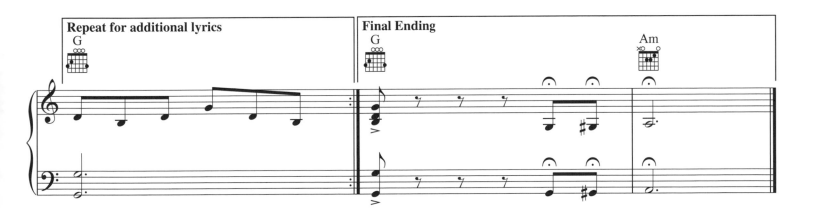

Additional Lyrics

When you walk around the world, babe,
You said you'd try to look for the end of the road.
You might find out later that the road'll end in Detroit,
Honey, the road'll even end in Katmandu.
You can go all around the world try'n' to find
Something to do with your life, babe,
When you only gotta do one thing well to make it in this world, babe:
You got a woman waitin' for you there,
All you ever gotta do is be a good man one time to one woman
And that'll be the end of the road, babe!
I know you got more tears to share, babe,
So come on, come on, come on and cry, cry baby, etc.

DO RIGHT WOMAN DO RIGHT MAN

Words and Music by DAN PENN
and CHIPS MOMAN

Take me to heart _____ and I'll al-ways love you, and no-bod-y _____ can

(Sittin' On)
THE DOCK OF THE BAY

Words and Music by STEVE CROPPER
and OTIS REDDING

EVERYBODY NEEDS SOMEBODY TO LOVE

Words and Music by BERT BERNS,
SOLOMAN BURKE and GERRY WEXLER

GEE WHIZ

Words and Music by
CARLA THOMAS

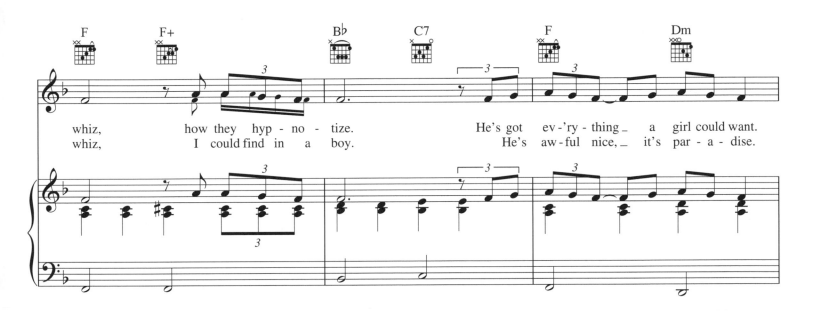

GREEN ONIONS

Written by AL JACKSON, JR., LEWIS STEINBERG,
BOOKER T. JONES and STEVE CROPPER

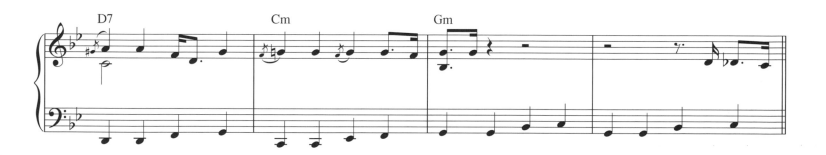

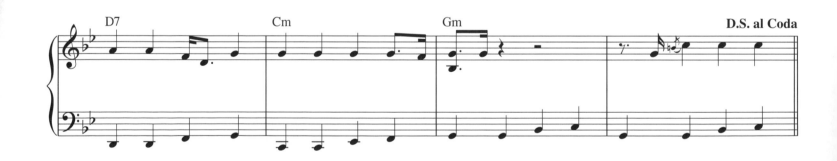

HARD TO HANDLE

Words and Music by ALLEN JONES,
ALVERTIS BELL and OTIS REDDING

Moderate Funk

N.C.

Bb7

1.,3. Ba - by, here I am ___ I'm a man on the scene. ___
2. *(See additional lyrics)*

I can give you what you want, _ but you got to go home _ with me.

I've got some good _ old lov - in' and I've got some in store. _

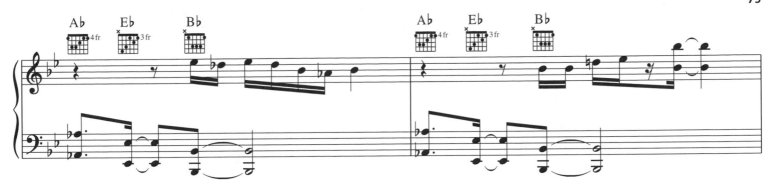

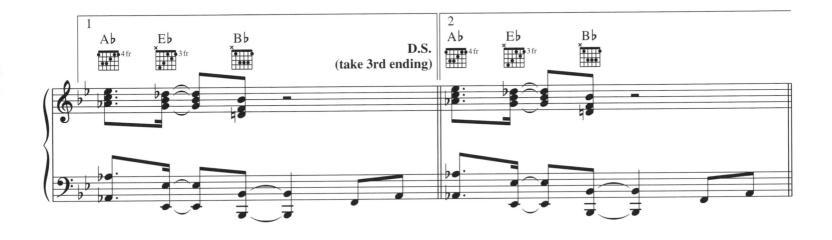

Additional Lyrics

2. Action speaks louder than words, and I'm a man with a great experience.
   I know you got you another man, but I can love you better than him.
   Take my hand, don't be afraid, I want to prove every word that I said.
   I'm advertising love for free, so won't you place your ad with me?
   Boys will come a dime by the dozen, but that ain't nothin' but kiss and look.
   Pretty little thing, let me light the candle, 'cause mama, I'm sure hard to handle, now.

HERE I AM, COME AND TAKE ME

Words and Music by AL GREEN
and MABON HODGES

I CAN'T STAND THE RAIN

Words and Music by DON BRYANT,
ANN PEEBLES and BERNARD MILLER

me.   Hey, win-dow-pane,   do you re-mem - ber

ries.   I can't stand the rain. *Instrumental*

ries.   I can't stand the rain   'gainst my win-dow

how sweet it used to be? ___   When we were to -

            Instrumental ends)

'cause he's not here with me. ___)   Whoa,   emp - ty

geth - er, huh, ___ huh,   ev -'ry-thing was so grand. ___   Yes, it was.

pil - low, huh, ___ huh,   where his head used to lay,   yeah.

(Your Love Keeps Lifting Me)
HIGHER AND HIGHER

Words and Music by GARY JACKSON,
CARL SMITH and RAYNARD MINER

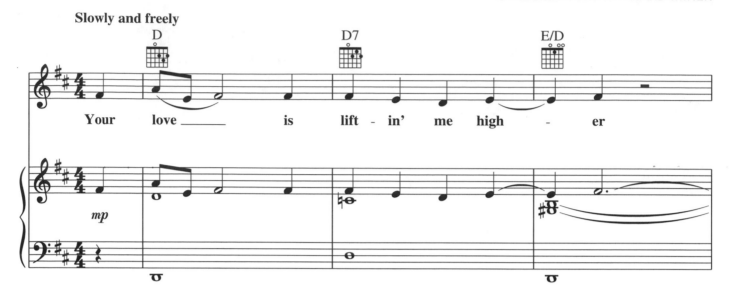

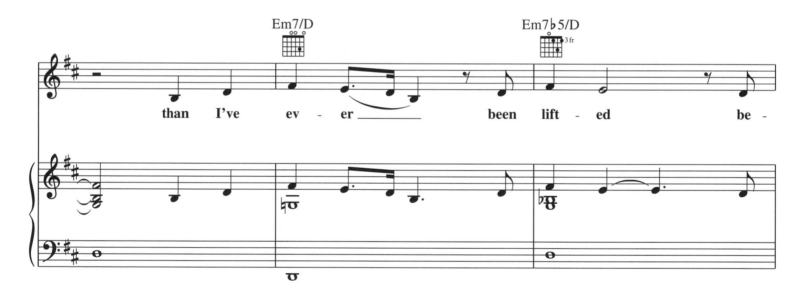

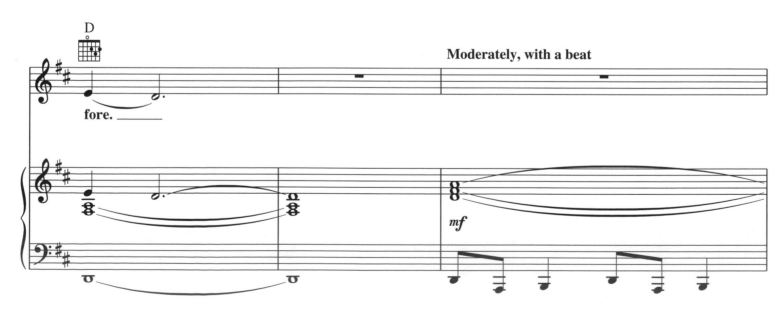

HOLD ON I'M COMIN'

Words and Music by ISAAC HAYES
and DAVID PORTER

I FORGOT TO BE YOUR LOVER

Words and Music by WILLIAM BELL
and BOOKER T. JONES, JR.

I GOT A SURE THING

Words and Music by WILLIAM BELL,
OLLIE HOSKINS and BOOKER T. JONES, JR.

I GOT YOU
(I Feel Good)

Words and Music by
JAMES BROWN

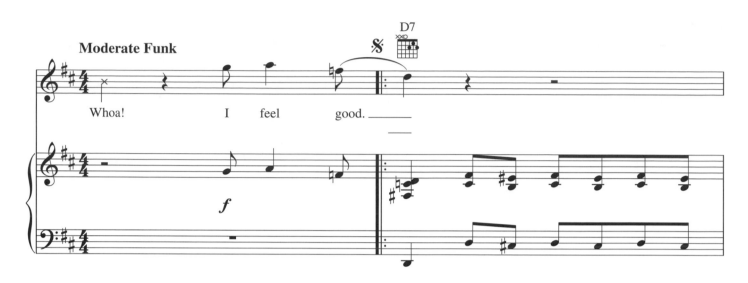

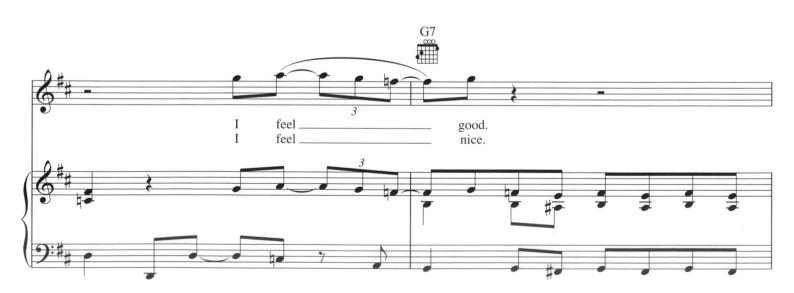

I LIKE WHAT YOU'RE DOING TO ME

Words and Music by HOMER BANKS,
BETTYE JEAN BARNES CRUTCHER and RAYMOND JACKSON

I HEARD IT THROUGH THE GRAPEVINE

Words and Music by NORMAN J. WHITFIELD
and BARRETT STRONG

D.S. al Coda

Peo - ple say be - lieve half ___

CODA

___ yeah, yeah, ___ yeah. I heard it through the grape - vine, not much

Repeat and Fade

long - er would you be mine, ba - by. Yeah, ___

I PITY THE FOOL

By DON ROBEY

fool. _____

Say, _____

_____ I pit - y the fool. _____

Whoa, _____ I _____

pit - y the fool. _____

I pit - y the

fool _____ that falls _____ in love with you.

He'll

He'll take your love __ a - way 'cause he found an - oth - er fool to play. __ That's why _____ I ___ pit - y the fool. __

Vocal ab lib.

Repeat and Fade

Optional Ending

I THANK YOU

Words and Music by ISAAC HAYES
and DAVID PORTER

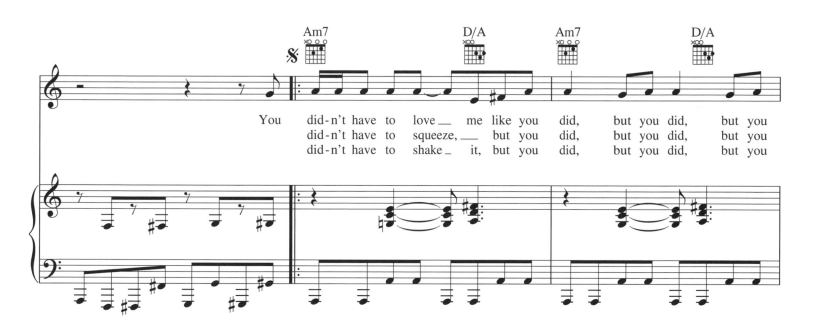

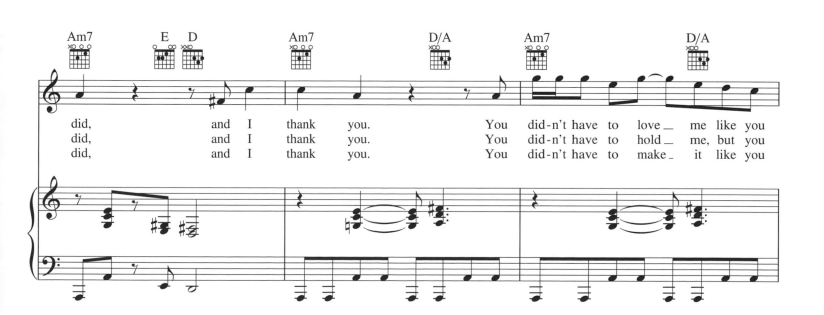

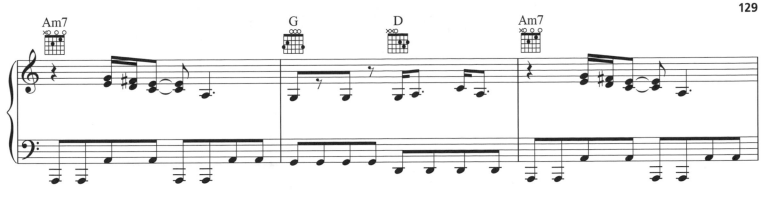

D.S. al Coda

You

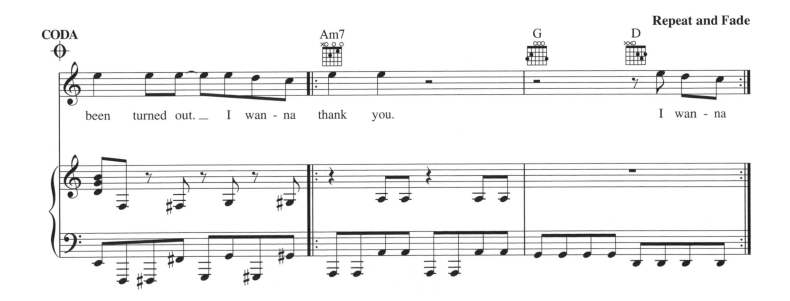

CODA

Repeat and Fade

been turned out. __ I wan - na thank you.

I wan - na

I WANT SOMEONE

Words and Music by ESTELLE AXTON
and WILLIA PARKER

I'LL BE THE OTHER WOMAN

Words and Music by HOMER BANKS
and CARL HAMPTON

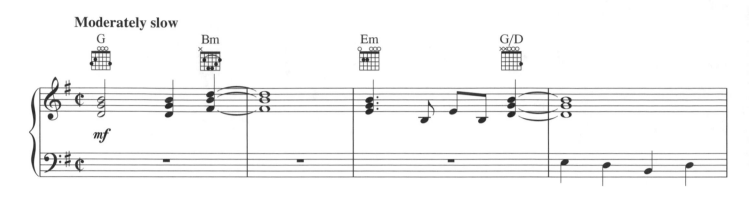

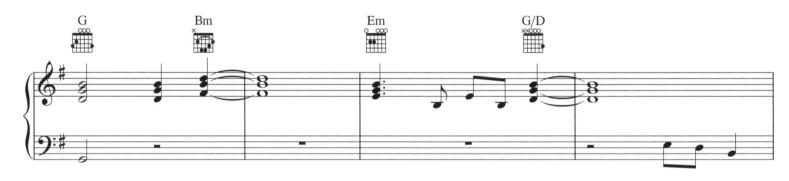

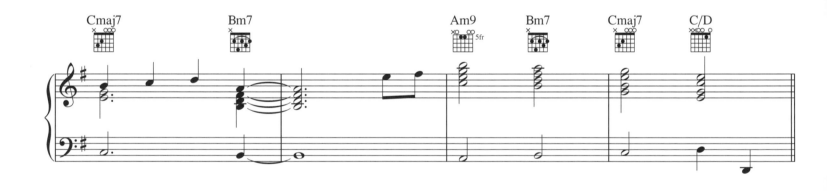

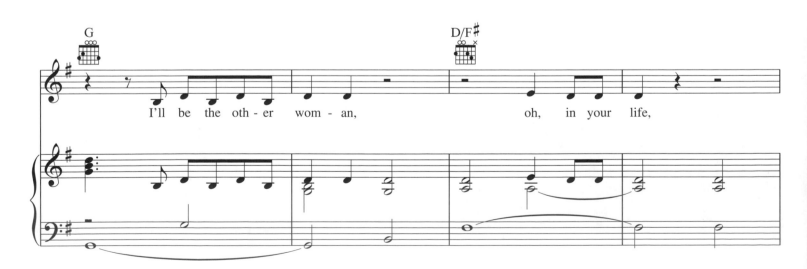

I'll be the oth-er wom-an,   oh, in your life,

And sec-ond to that ___ I'll be. ___ But when ___ you're not

there with her, ___ I want you right here with me. ___

I'll be the oth-er wom — an just as long as I

know I'm the on-ly oth-er wom — an that you

I'M GONNA TEAR YOUR PLAYHOUSE DOWN

Words and Music by
EARL RANDLE

I'LL TAKE YOU THERE

Words and Music by
ALVERTIS ISBELL

I'VE BEEN LONELY
(For So Long)

Words and Music by POSIE KNIGHT
and JERRY WEAVER

I'VE BEEN LOVING YOU TOO LONG

Words and Music by OTIS REDDING
and JERRY BUTLER

1. I've been lov-ing you _____
2. (See additional lyrics)

too long ___ to stop now. ___

You are tired _____ and you

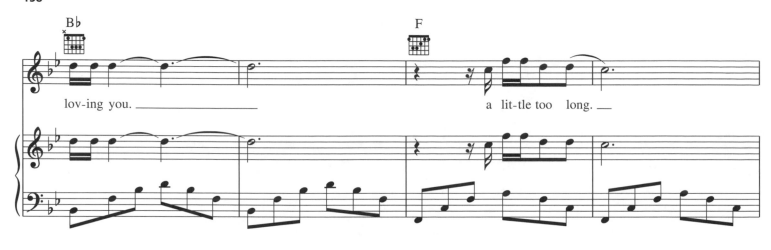

Additional Lyrics

2. With you, my life has been so wonderful;
I can't stop now.
You are tired,
And your love is growing cold;
My love is growing stronger,
As our affair grows old.
I've been loving you, a little too long;
I don't wanna stop now.

IN THE MIDNIGHT HOUR

Words and Music by STEVE CROPPER
and WILSON PICKETT

hold you, and do all the things I told you in the mid-night

hour. Yes, I am, oh yes, I am.

I'm gon-na wait 'til stars come out _____ and see that

twin-kle in your eyes. I'm gon-na wait 'til the mid-night hour, that's when my

I'VE NEVER FOUND A GIRL
(To Love Me like You Do)

Words and Music by ALVERTIS ISBELL,
EDDIE FLOYD and BOOKER T. JONES, JR.

you do. ___

Ain't no

No, I ain't

nev - er, nev - er found me a girl   to love me like   you do,

IN THE RAIN

Words and Music by
ANTHONY HESTER

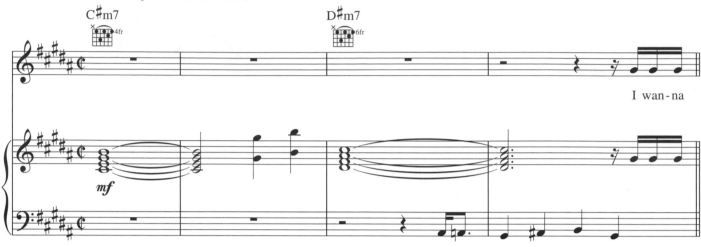

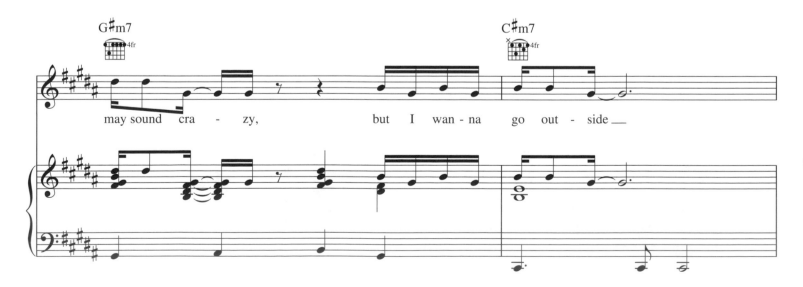

Knock On Wood

Words and Music by EDDIE FLOYD
and STEVE CROPPER

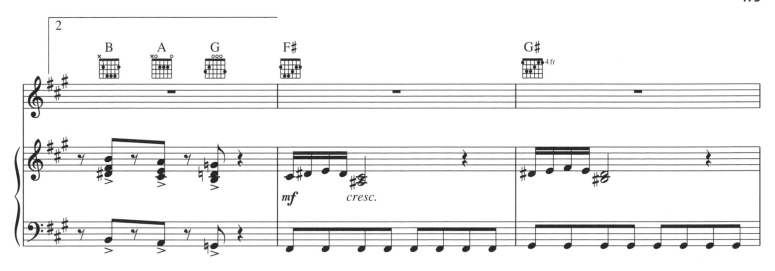

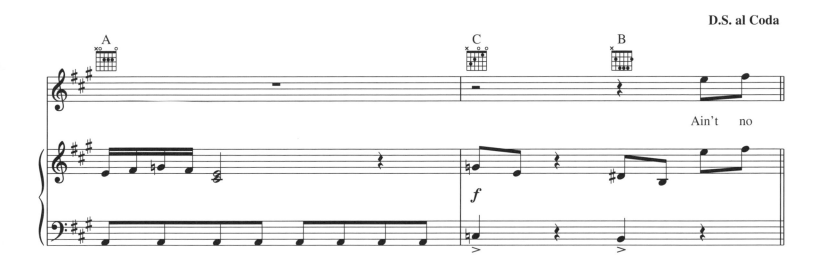

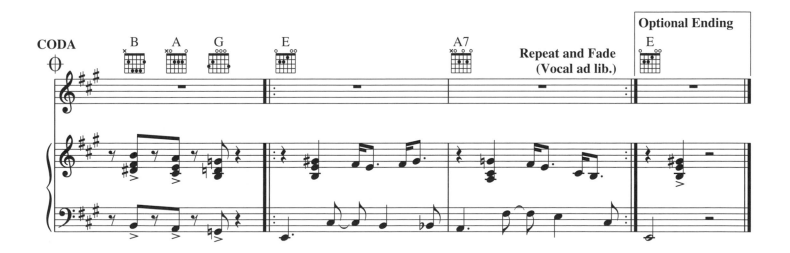

Additional Lyrics

3. Ain't no secret that a woman can feel my love come up.
You got me seeing, she really sees that, that I get enough.
Just one touch from you, baby, you know it means so much.
It's like thunder, lightning;
The way you love me is frightening,
I think I better knock knock knock knock on wood.

JUMP BACK

Words and Music by
RUFUS THOMAS

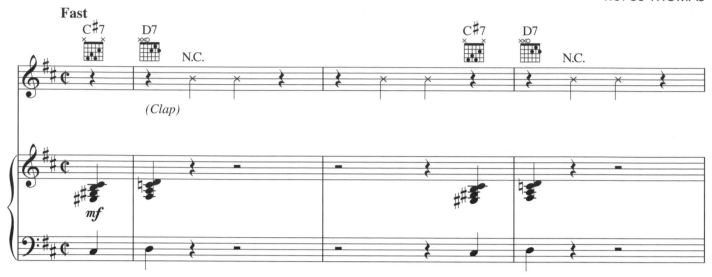

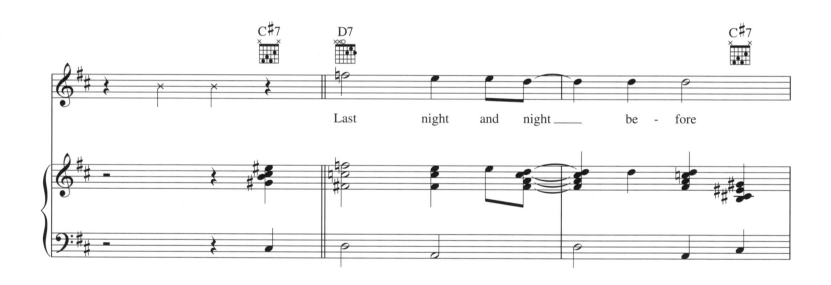

JUST ONE LOOK

Words and Music by DORIS PAYNE
and GREGORY CARROLL

LET'S GET IT ON

Words and Music by MARVIN GAYE
and ED TOWNSEND

Slow Soul beat

I've been real-ly try - in', ba - by, try-in' to hold _ back this feel-

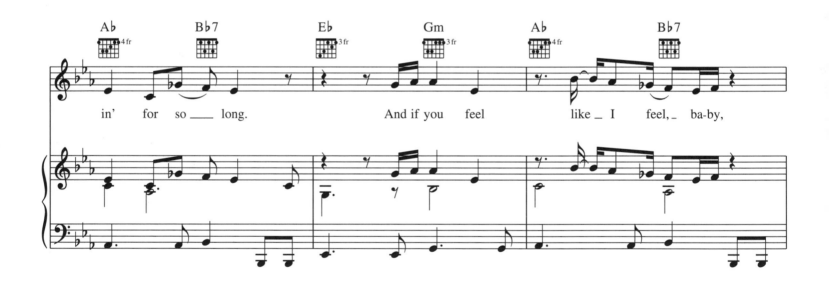

in' for so _ long. And if you feel like _ I feel, _ ba-by,

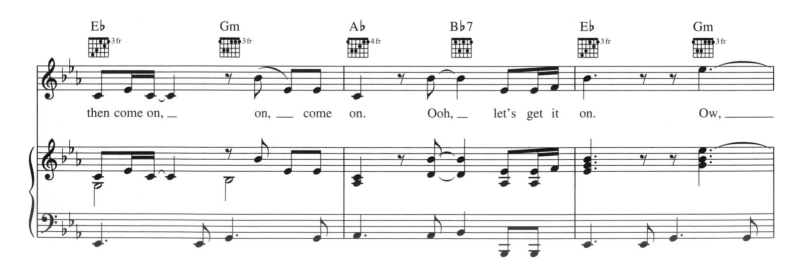

then come on, _ on, _ come on. Ooh, _ let's get it on. Ow, _

LAST NIGHT

Words and Music by CHARLES AXTON,
GILBERT CAPLE, CHIPS MOMAN,
FLOYD NEWMAN and JERRY SMITH

Moderate 12-bar Blues

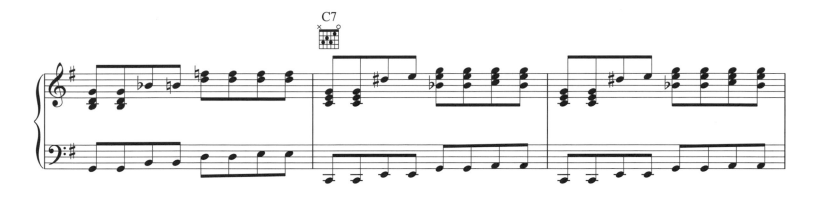

Oh, _____ last night!

LET ME BE GOOD TO YOU

Words and Music by CARL WELLS,
DAVID PORTER and ISAAC HAYES

LET'S STAY TOGETHER

Words and Music by AL GREEN,
WILLIE MITCHELL and AL JACKSON, JR.

LIVING FOR THE CITY

Words and Music by
STEVIE WONDER

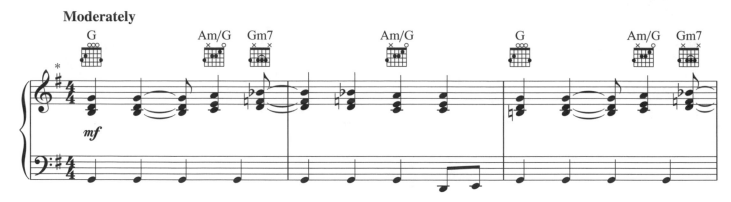

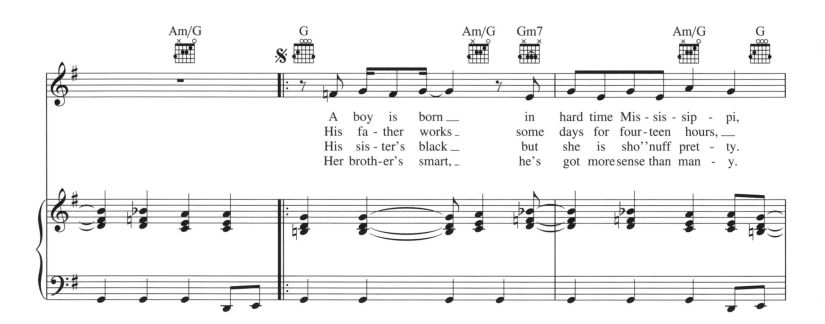

A boy is born ___ in hard time Mis-sis-sip-pi,
His fa-ther works ___ some days for four-teen hours, ___
His sis-ter's black ___ but she is sho''nuff pret-ty.
Her broth-er's smart, ___ he's got more sense than man-y.

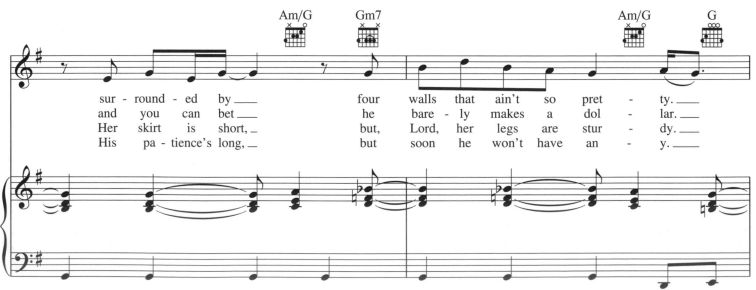

sur-round-ed by ___ four walls that ain't so pret-ty. ___
and you can bet ___ he bare-ly makes a dol-lar. ___
Her skirt is short, ___ but, Lord, her legs are stur-dy. ___
His pa-tience's long, ___ but soon he won't have an-y. ___

Recorded a half step lower.

MR. BIG STUFF

Words and Music by JOSEPH BROUSSARD,
RALPH WILLIAMS and CARROL WASHINGTON

LONELY TEARDROPS

Words and Music by BERRY GORDY,
GWEN GORDY FUQUA and TYRAN CARLO

Lone - ly tear - drops, my pil - low's

nev - er dry. __ Lone - ly tear - drops, come

MR. PITIFUL

Words and Music by OTIS REDDING
and STEVE CROPPER

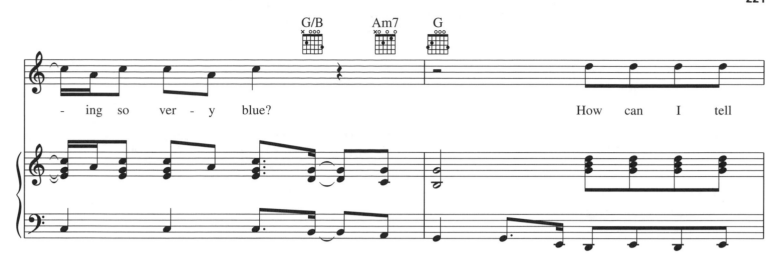

- ing so ver - y blue? How can I tell

you 'bout my fame? Oh, _____ don't think t'will do. Yeah, Mis - ter _

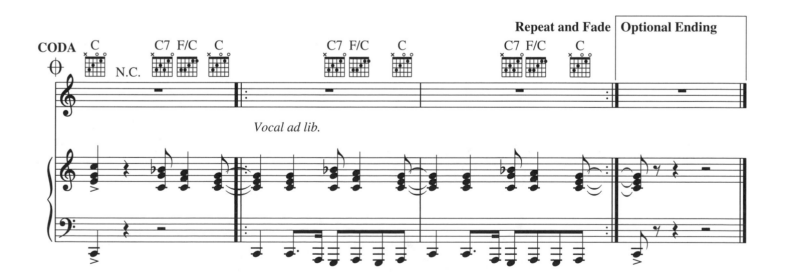

Vocal ad lib.

Additional Lyrics

2. They call me Mr. Pitiful; yes, everybody knows, now.
They call me Mr. Pitiful most every place I go.
But nobody seems to understand, now, what makes a man sing such a sad song,
When he lost everything, when he lost everything he had.

MUSTANG SALLY

Words and Music by
BONNY RICE

Moderate Blues Rock

Mus - tang Sal - ly.

Think you bet - ter slow your mus - tang down.

Mus - tang

All you want to do is ride a-round, Sal-ly. Ride, Sal-ly, ride.__

All you want to do is ride a-round, Sal-ly. Ride, Sal-ly, ride._

All you want to do is ride a-round, Sal-ly.

To Coda

(You Make Me Feel Like)
A NATURAL WOMAN

Words and Music by GERRY GOFFIN,
CAROLE KING and JERRY WEXLER

NEVER CAN SAY GOODBYE

Words and Music by
CLIFTON DAVIS

tried and tried to hide __ my feel - ings, they al - ways seem to show. __ Then you
ver - y strange vi - bra - tion pierc - ing me right to the core. __ It says,
same un - hap - py feel - ing that __ there's that an - guish, there's that doubt. __ It's the

try to say __ you're leav - ing me, __ and I al - ways have __ to say, "No, __ tell me
"Turn a - round, __ you fool. __ You know you love her more __ and more." __ Tell me
same old diz - zy hang - up; can't __ do with you or __ with - out. __ Tell me

To Coda

why __ is it so?" __ But I __
why __ is it so? __ Don't wan - na let you go. __
why __ is it so? __

I nev - er can say good-bye, __ girl. I nev - er can say good-bye,

PAPA'S GOT A BRAND NEW BAG

Words and Music by
JAMES BROWN

Moderate Funk

Come here, sis - ter,
ma - ma,

Pa - pa's in the swing.
and dig this cra - zy scene.

He ain't too
He's not too

hip
fan - cy

a - bout that new breed, babe.
but this line is pret - ty clean.

PATCHES

Words and Music by GENERAL JOHNSON
and RONALD DUNBAR

(Spoken:)
I was born and raised in Alabama, on a farm way back up in the woods.
Then one day a strong rain came and

washed all the crops away.
I was so ragged that folks used to call me "Patches."
And at the age of thirteen I thought I was

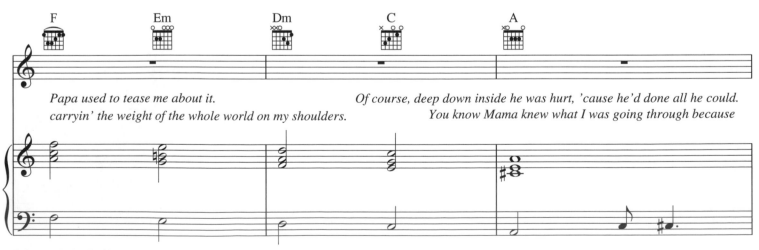

Papa used to tease me about it.
carryin' the weight of the whole world on my shoulders.

Of course, deep down inside he was hurt, 'cause he'd done all he could.
You know Mama knew what I was going through because

* *Recorded a half step lower.*

A RAINY NIGHT IN GEORGIA

Words and Music by
TONY JOE WHITE

1. Hov - erin' by my suit - case, tryin' to find a warm place to
2. Ne - on signs a-flash - in', tax - i - cabs and bus - es pass - in'
3. *(See additional lyrics)*

spend the night; a heav - y rain a-fall - in';
through the night; the dis - tant moan - in' of a train

seems I hear your voice call - in', "It's all right."
seems to play a sad re - frain to the night:

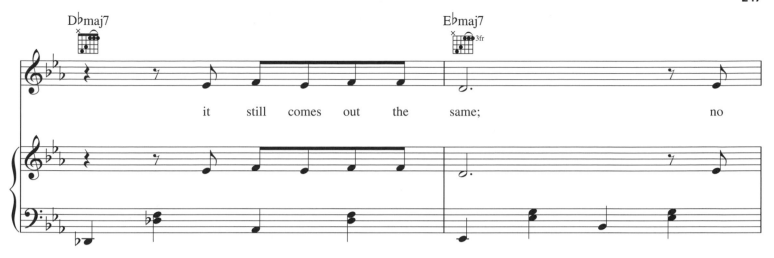

it still comes out the same; no

mat- ter how you look at it, think of it, you

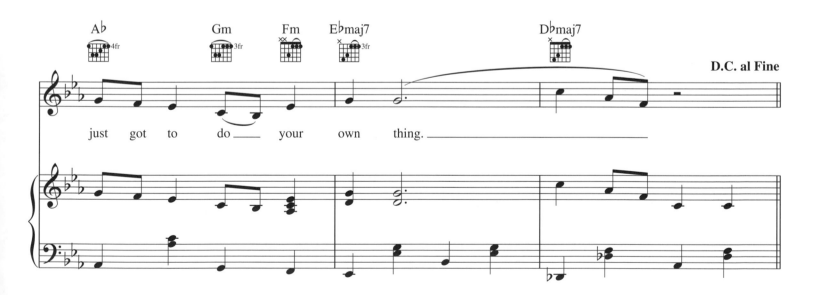

just got to do ___ your own thing. _____

D.C. al Fine

Additional Lyrics

3. I find me a place in a box car,
   So I take out my guitar to pass some time;
   Late at night when it's hard to rest,
   I hold your picture to my chest, and I'm all right.
   Chorus

PRIVATE NUMBER

Words and Music by BOOKER T. JONES
and WILLIAM BELL

Since I've been gone, __
I'm sor - ry you could - n't

__ you've had __ your num - ber changed. __
call me __ when you got home. __

But my love for you, __ girl, still __ re - mains the same. __
But oth - er fel - las kept __ on call - in' while you were gone. __

RESPECT

Words and Music by
OTIS REDDING

Ooh, __ your kiss - es, (ooh) sweet-er than hon - ey.

(Ooh) And guess what? (Ooh) So is my mon - ey. (Ooh) All I want you to

do for me is give it to me when you get home, yeah, ba - by, whip it to me
(Ooh) (Re - re - re - re - re - re - re - re - re - re - re-

THEME FROM SHAFT

from SHAFT

Words and Music by
ISAAC HAYES

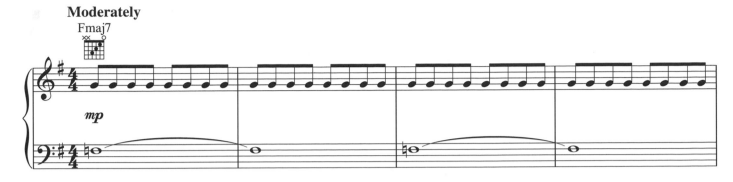

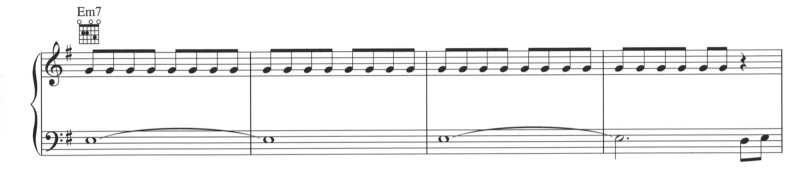

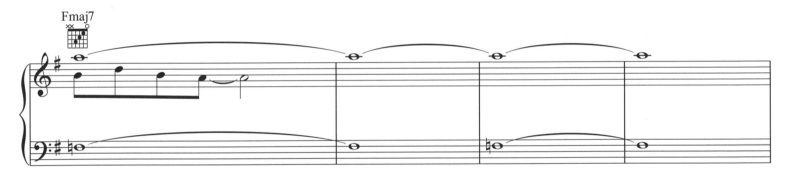

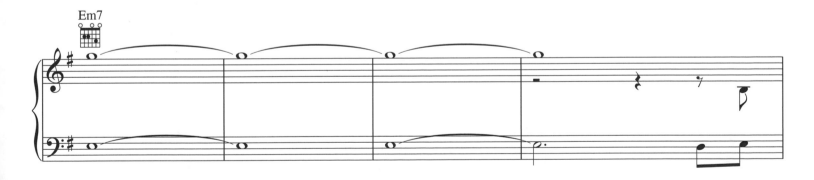

(Spoken:) Who's the black pri-vate dick ___ that's a sex ma-chine to all the chicks?   (Shaft!)

You're damn right!

Who   is the man   that would risk his life for his broth-er man? _   (Shaft!)

no one un-der-stands him but his wom-an. (John   Shaft!)

RESPECT YOURSELF

Words and Music by MACK RICE
and LUTHER INGRAM

don't give a heck a-bout the man with the Bi-ble in his hand,
talk-in' 'bout the pres-i-dent won't stop air pol-lu-tion.

just get out the way and let the gen-tle-man do his thing.
Put your hand o'er your mouth when you cough that-'ll help the so-lu-

tion. Oh, __ you cuss a-round wom-en folk,

You the kind of gen-tle-man

want ev-'ry-thing your way. __
don't e-ven know their name. __

Take the
Then you're

sheet off   your face,   boy.   It's a brand-new   day. ___
dumb e-nough to think   it-'ll   make_   you a   big ol'   man.

Re-spect your-self. ___   Re-spect your-self. ___

Re-spect your-self. ___   Re-spect your-self. ___

G7

If you don't re-spect your-self, ain't no-bod-y   gon-na give a good, good

SIXTY MINUTE MAN

Words and Music by WILLIAM WARD
and ROSE MARKS

SOUL MAN

Words and Music by ISAAC HAYES
and DAVID PORTER

Com-in' to you on a dust-y road, good lov-in' I got a truck-load. And

what I got on the hard way and I'll make it bet-ter each and ev-'ry day.

brought up on a side street. I learned how to love be-fore I could eat. I was

SOUL SERENADE

Words and Music by CURTIS OUSLEY
and LUTHER DIXON

THINK

Words and Music by ARETHA FRANKLIN
and TED WHITE

You bet - ter think, think a - bout what you're tryin' to do to me. __ Think, let your mind go, let your - self be free. __ Let's go back, __ let's go back, let's go

TIRED OF BEING ALONE

Words and Music by
AL GREEN

I'm so tired ___ of be-ing a - lone, I'm so tired ___ of on my own, won't you

help me, girl, ___ just as soon ___ as you can? ___

Peo - ple say ___ that I found a way to make you say ___ that you
I guess you know that I love you so ___ e - ven though ___ you don't

love _____ me.
You did - n't go for that,

want me _ no more. _____
Now I'm cry - in' tears,

it's a nat - 'ral fact,
that I wan-na come back;
show me where it's at. _____

all _ through the years,
I'll tell you like it is;
love me if you will. _____

_____ Ba - by.
I'm so tired _ _____

TRAMP

Words and Music by LOWELL FULSOM
and JIMMY McCRACKLIN

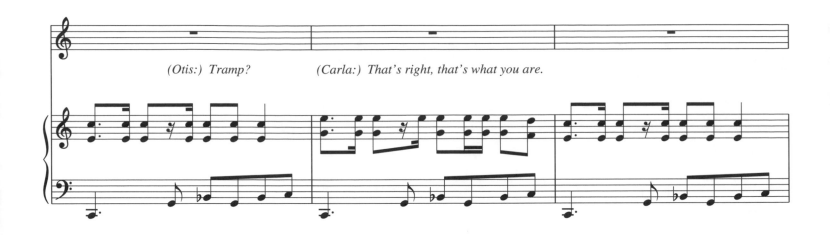

(Otis:) Tramp?   (Carla:) That's right, that's what you are.

G7   F7   C

D.C. al Coda
(see Additional Lyrics)

Optional Ending
Repeat and Fade
(Ad lib. dialogue)

CODA   C7   C

Additional Lyrics

Carla: You know what, Otis, I don't care what you say,
You're still a tramp.

Otis: What?

That's right, you don't even have a fat bankroll
in your pocket. You probably haven't even got
twenty-five cents.

I got six Cadillacs, five Lincolns, four Olds,
six Mercurys, three T-Birds, a Mustang...
To Chorus:

WHAT A MAN

Words and Music by
DAVID CRAWFORD

UP THE LADDER TO THE ROOF

Words and Music by
VINCENT DiMIRCO

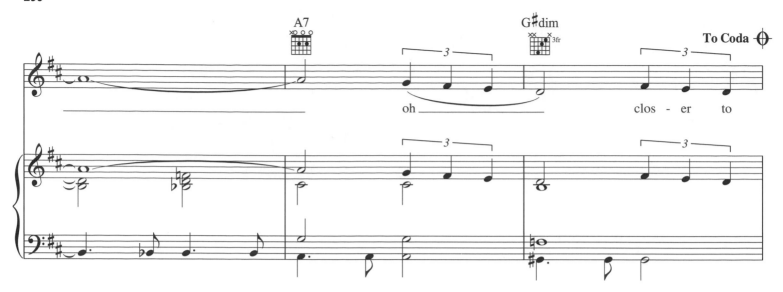

oh _____ clos - er to

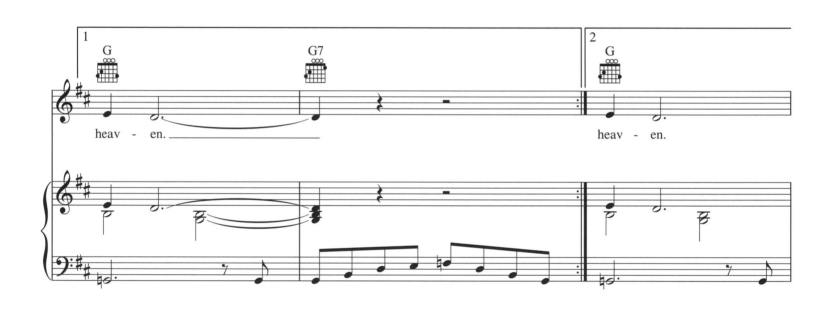

heav - en. _____ heav - en.

We'll laugh _ and I'll   tell you the sto - ry of love _

I will _ nev - er   ev - er ev - er _ leave ___

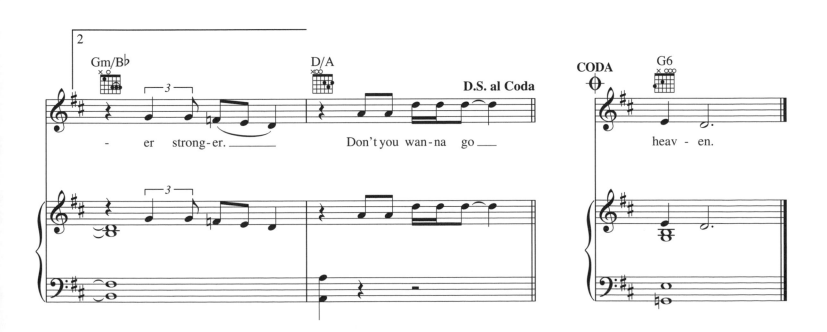

WALK ON BY

Lyric by HAL DAVID
Music by BURT BACHARACH

If you see me walk-in' down the street and I start to cry ____ each time we meet, ____
I just can't get o - ver los - in' you and so if I seem ____ bro - ken and blue, ____

walk on by, ____ walk on by. ____

Make be - lieve ____ that you don't see the tears. Just let me grieve ____ in
Fool - ish pride, ____ that's all that I have left, so let me hide ____ the

WHAT'D I SAY

Words and Music by
RAY CHARLES

WOMAN TO WOMAN

Words and Music by EDDIE MARION,
JAMES BANKS and HENDERSON THIGPEN, JR.

Hello,   may I speak to Barbara?

Barbara, this is Shirley.   You might not know who I am. But, the reason I'm callin' is because
You see, it doesn't really make any difference.   But it's only fair that I let you know that the man you're in love with

I was goin' through my old man's pockets this mornin'   and I just happened to find your name and number.
he's mine,   from the top of his head to the bottom of his feet,   the bed he sleeps in and every piece of food he eats.

WHAT'S GOING ON

Words and Music by MARVIN GAYE,
AL CLEVELAND and RENALDO BENSON

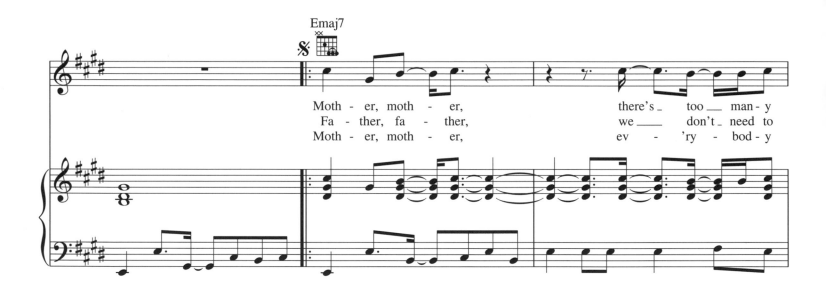

Moth-er, moth-er, there's _ too _ man-y
Fa-ther, fa-ther, we __ don't _ need to
Moth-er, moth-er, ev- 'ry- bod- y

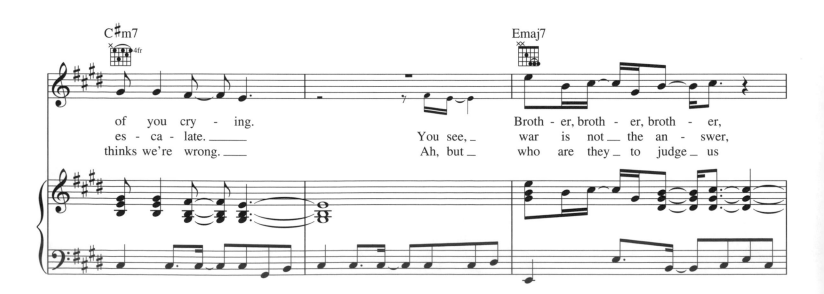

of you cry- ing.
es - ca- late. _____
thinks we're wrong. ___

Broth- er, broth- er, broth- er,
You see, _ war is not _ the an - swer,
Ah, but _ who are they _ to judge _ us

WHEN SOMETHING IS WRONG WITH MY BABY

Words and Music by ISAAC HAYES
and DAVID PORTER

Moderately slow

* Recorded a half step higher.

WHO'S MAKING LOVE

Words and Music by BETTYE CRUTCHER,
DON DAVIS, HOMER BANKS
and RAYMOND JACKSON

YOUR GOOD THING
(Is About to End)

Words and Music by DAVID PORTER
and ISAAC HAYES

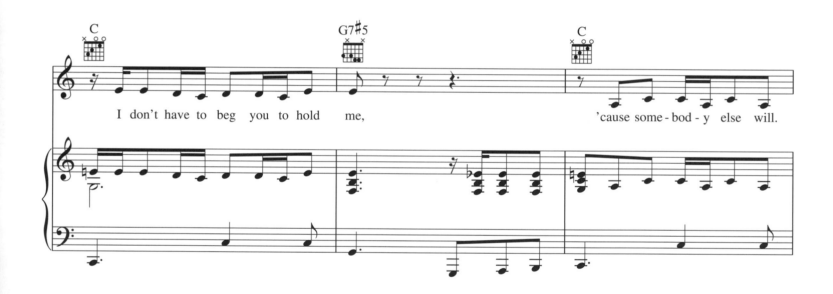

I don't have to beg you to hold me,   'cause some-bod-y else will.

You don't have to love me when I want it

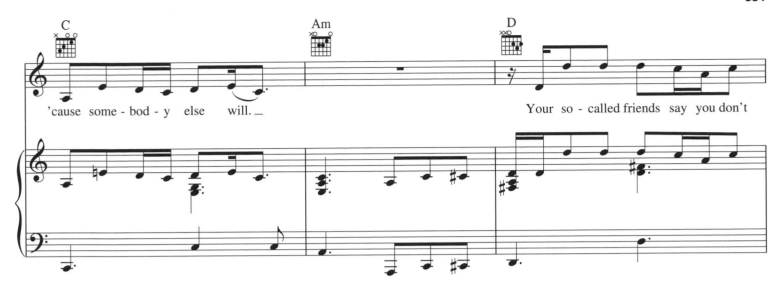

'cause some - bod - y else will. __ Your so - called friends say you don't

need it. But all the time, they're try'n' to get it. Look out.

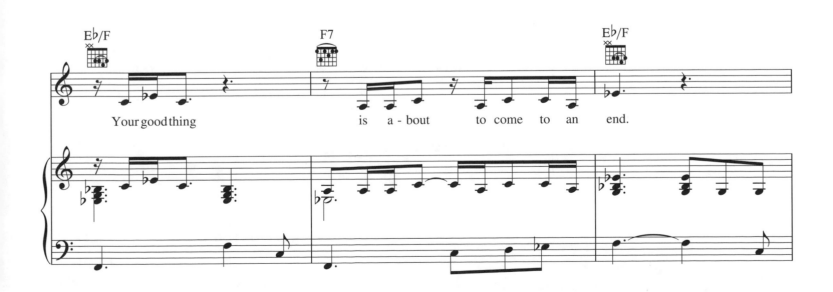

Your good thing is a - bout to come to an end.

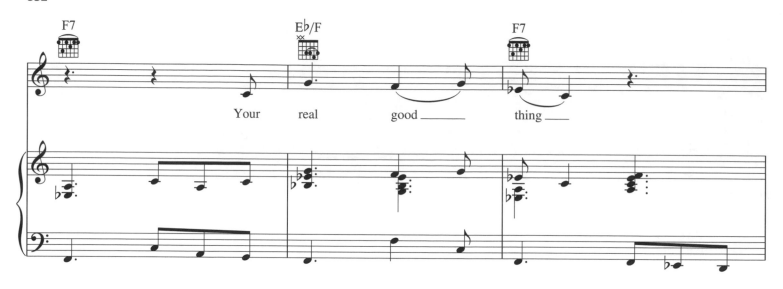

Your real good _____ thing _____

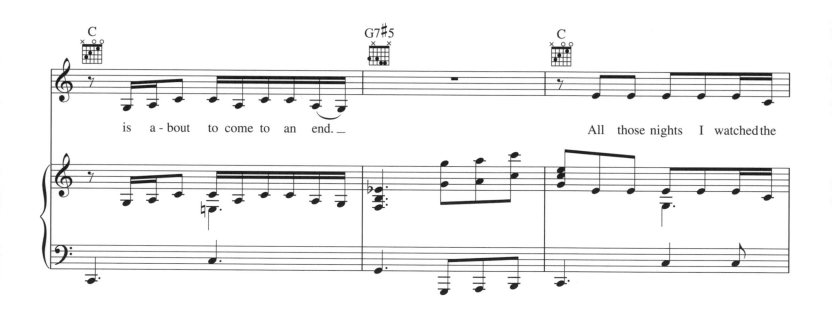

is a-bout to come to an end. _____ All those nights I watched the

four walls, I did-n't have to watch 'em all a-lone.

When oth- er men said they want- ed me, I did- n't have to tell them I was your _

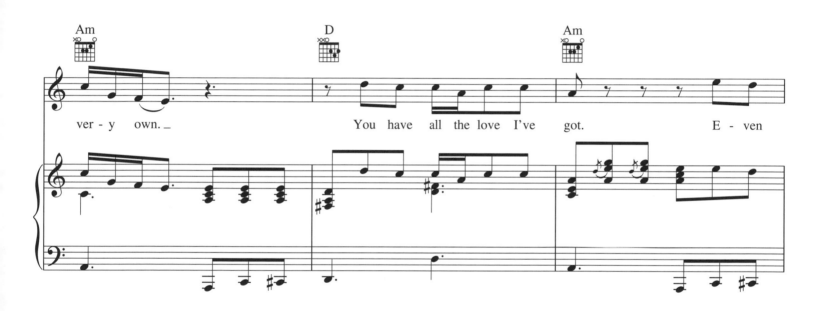

ver- y own. _ You have all the love I've got. E - ven

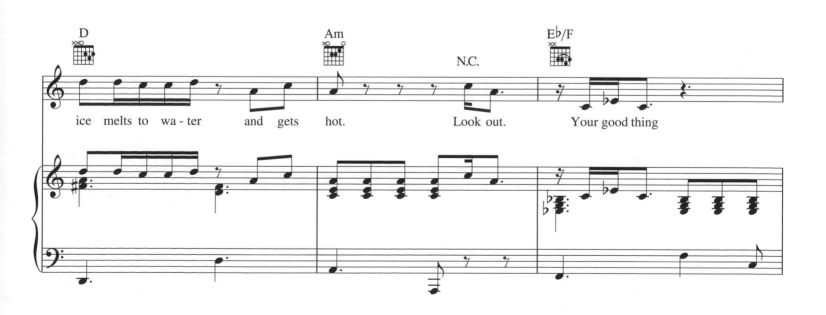

ice melts to wa- ter and gets hot. Look out. Your good thing

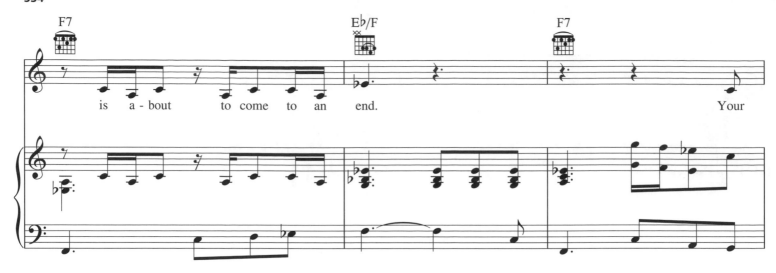

is a - bout to come to an end. Your

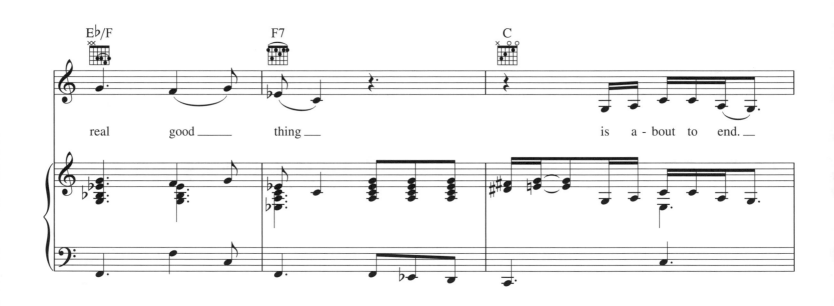

real good _____ thing _____ is a - bout to end. ___

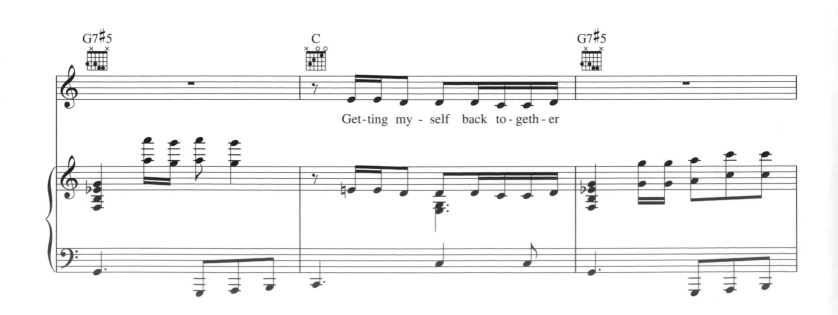

Get - ting my - self back to - geth - er

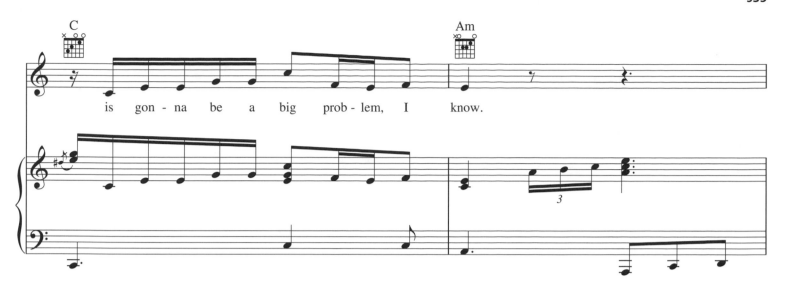

is gon - na be a big prob - lem, I know.

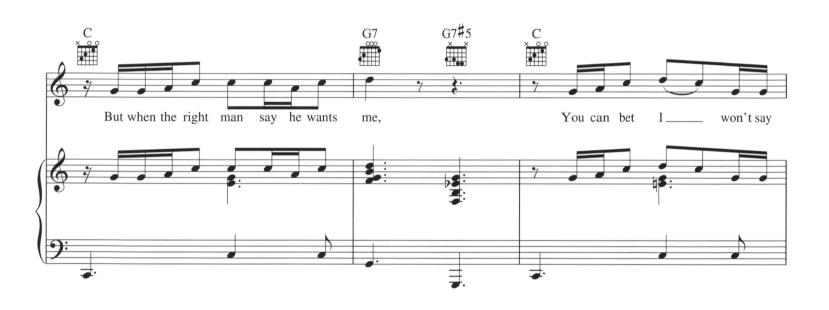

But when the right man say he wants me, You can bet I _____ won't say

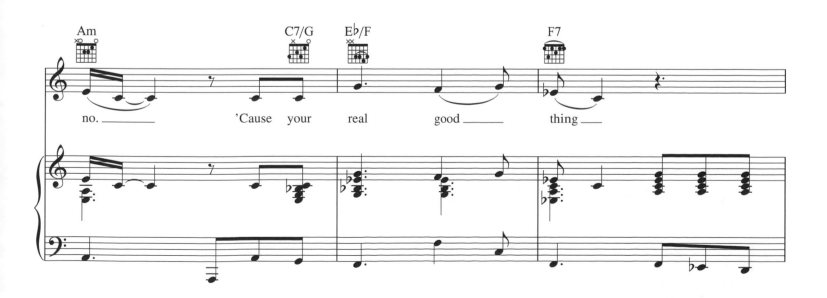

no. _____ 'Cause your real good _____ thing _____

is a-bout to end. __ Your real, _____ your

good thing, __ your good thing, ba - by, __ your good thing, __ mm, __ your good thing.

Optional Ending

Repeat and Fade

(Vocal ad lib.)